To Market,
To Market

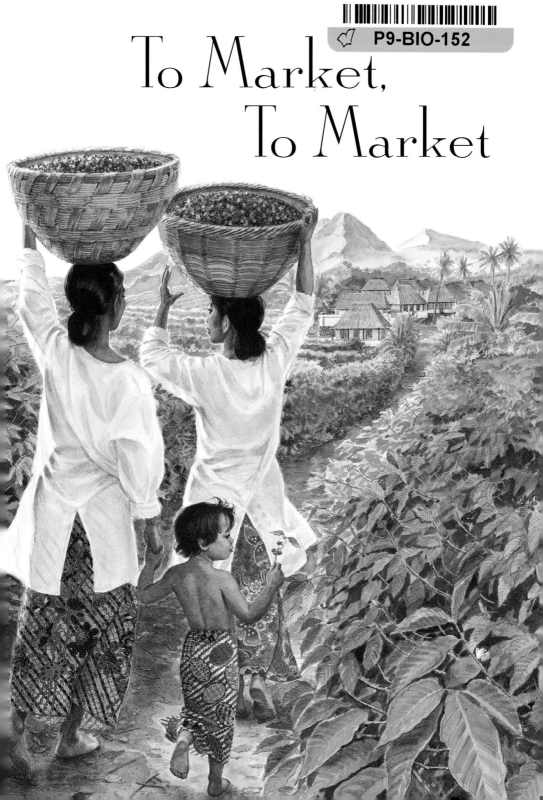

Contents

Features

Do you know which animals are sometimes called the "ships of the desert"? Check your answer on page 9.

Turn to page 11 to find out how Chinese traders used to keep track of their money.

TIME LINK

TECHTALK

The famous Panama Canal is built across land that is not level. To find out how boats move from one level to another, turn to page 19.

Pick up your shopping list and take a closer look at markets around the world in **Let's Go Shopping!** on page 20.

IN FOCUS

SITESEEING · PAST & FUTURE ·

Which country first made paper money?

Visit **www.rigbyinfoquest.com** for more about **TRADING.**

Early Trading

When our pantry is bare, we make a short trip to the supermarket. However, it wasn't always so easy for people to gain what they needed.

Long ago, people were **hunters and gatherers.** They moved around, looking for food. Then people began to settle in villages. They planted the seeds of wild fruit and vegetables. They herded animals for food and made clothes from the animals' skins. Soon they started to trade with people in other villages.

Hunters and gatherers often had to travel long distances to find food and other things they needed.

In many places today, people can order goods by using a computer at home.

The First Towns

The first great towns of the world grew along rivers in Egypt and an area called Sumer, now southeastern Iraq. People **invented** systems of writing and mathematics to keep records of their trading. They invented the wheel, the plow, and ways of **irrigating** the dry desert soil in order to grow better crops. They made laws to control their towns.

The first markets in Egypt did not use money. The weight of the goods was also their price. 1 pound of pottery could be traded for 1 pound of vegetables.

EUROPE

Mediterranean Sea

• Sumer

Egypt

Persian Gulf

Arabia

Nile River

Red Sea

AFRICA

INDIAN OCEAN

Trading Grows

Over 5,000 years ago, Egyptians invented sails to replace oars in powering their boats. This let them trade with countries farther away. Soon, other countries also used large sailing ships to travel to more markets.

Merchants traveled from near and far to **barter** for goods. Traders from Europe brought furs, cloth, and **manufactured goods.** Traders from India brought gold, jewels, and spices. Goods were checked carefully before being loaded onto boats or camels.

The busy market of Baghdad in Persia was an important meeting place for traders from Europe and Asia.

Camels have often been called "ships of the desert." Camels can go without food or water for a long time. Merchants traveling with a group of camels, called a caravan, carried goods between Europe, Asia, and Africa across the deserts of Persia and Arabia.

The Silk Road

Trade routes began to connect towns. Travelers and traders went to far-off countries to find different goods to buy and sell. One important product was silk.

The trade routes to China became known as the Silk Road. The Silk Road became a highway for goods, ideas, information, and skills. Camel caravans carrying silk from China crossed the Gobi Desert and used roads leading to the coasts.

Traders often sold their goods to travelers they met on the Silk Road. The travelers then took the goods back to their own markets.

ASIA

Gobi Desert

Baghdad

China

India

Arabia

—— The Silk Road

TIME LINK

Ancient Chinese coins had holes in the middle so they could be carried on strings. This made it easier for Chinese traders to keep track of large sums of money.

Merchants and Markets

Trade grew quickly during the years 1100 to 1453, a time called the **Middle Ages.** Merchants became powerful and wealthy.

Sea transportation was still the most important way of getting goods to markets. Cities and countries joined together to form trading groups. If a town refused to join the trading group, its merchants were not allowed into port to load their ships or trade.

Goods were stored below the decks of ships to be kept safe and dry.

As trading grew, merchants found it dangerous to carry money between towns, so banks were set up where people could deposit money. Today, computerized banking makes it easy to move money around the world.

Between Two Worlds

The race was now on to find new trading routes. In 1492, Christopher Columbus set sail from Europe to find a new route to Asia. He did not find Asia, but he did connect the Eastern and Western parts of the world. Soon trading ships were traveling between the Old World of Europe and the New World of the Americas.

However, there were problems along this new trade route. Ships full of goods from the New World were often attacked and robbed by pirates.

The Europeans took horses, sheep, pigs, wheat, sugarcane, carts, iron, and steel to the New World. They returned to Europe with potatoes, pineapples, avocados, tomatoes, corn, vanilla, peanuts, turkeys, cocoa, rubber, timber, gold, and silver.

Some people of the New World slept in hanging beds called harmocas. Columbus' sailors copied this idea. They made these beds on their ships to sleep away from the rats. They called the beds hammocks.

Transportation Change

Trading is not possible without transportation. At first, people could only trade what they could carry. Then they began to use animals and wagons to move bigger loads. Slowly, shipping began to move **freight** between countries. This brought new goods to markets and spread people's ideas and knowledge.

The invention of engine-powered vehicles, such as trains, in the 1800s meant that goods could be carried faster and farther. Changes in transportation have changed where and how people trade.

Trucks bring freight to a dock. The freight is then put onto large ships. Moving freight by ship can be slow, but it is also the cheapest transportation over long distances.

Transporting goods by plane is the fastest way to move freight. However, it also costs the most.

Connecting the World

World trade has kept growing and changing over the years. In England during the 1800s, goods began to be made quickly and cheaply, but ships still had to carry their freight long distances around the world.

In 1869, a narrow waterway called the Suez Canal was opened to connect the Mediterranean and Red Seas. It shortened the sea route between Europe and India by 6,000 miles, making the world seem much smaller.

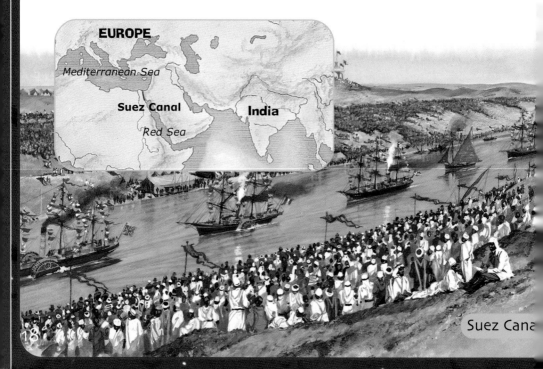

EUROPE

Mediterranean Sea

Suez Canal

India

Red Sea

Suez Cana

18

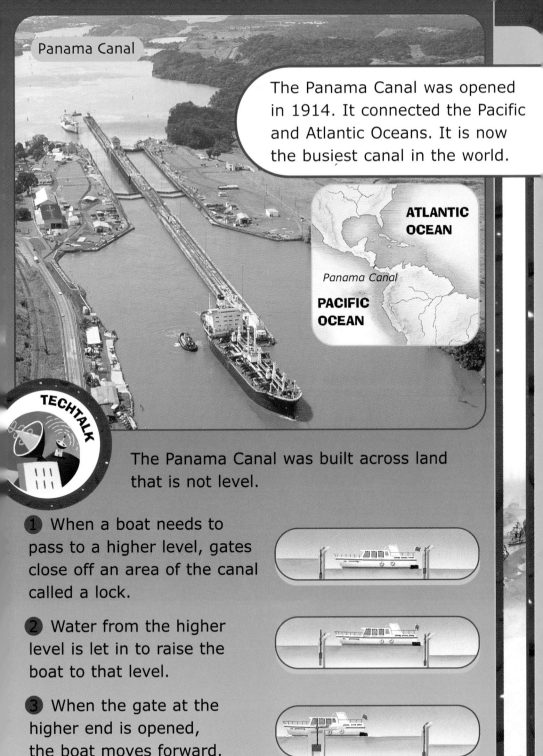

Panama Canal

The Panama Canal was opened in 1914. It connected the Pacific and Atlantic Oceans. It is now the busiest canal in the world.

ATLANTIC OCEAN

Panama Canal

PACIFIC OCEAN

TECHTALK

The Panama Canal was built across land that is not level.

1 When a boat needs to pass to a higher level, gates close off an area of the canal called a lock.

2 Water from the higher level is let in to raise the boat to that level.

3 When the gate at the higher end is opened, the boat moves forward.

IN FOCUS

Let's Go Shopping!

Shopping List

- ✔ French bread
- rice
- ✔ mangoes
- ✔ oranges
- ✔ olives
- ✔ tomatoes
- sugar
- ✔ spices
- coffee

Today at a supermarket, you can buy food from around the world. Have you ever thought about where the things at the supermarket may have come from?

World Production of Sugar, Coffee, and Rice

Sugar Production

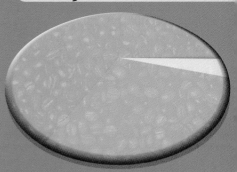

Coffee Production

Rice Production

Key to World Production

◯ U.S.A.	● Australia
● China	◯ Brazil
◯ India	◯ Rest of World

Glossary

barter – to trade goods without using money

freight – goods carried by truck, train, ship, or airplane

hunters and gatherers – people who lived by hunting animals and gathering wild plants. Hunters and gatherers moved from place to place.

invent – to think up an original, or new, product or process

irrigating – bringing water to the land to help crops grow. Early irrigation systems were often ditches with water flowing from a river to a crop.

manufactured goods – objects and materials, such as cloth, that have been made by people using their hands or machines

merchant – a person who buys and sells goods. Merchants are also called traders.

Middle Ages – the name for a period of time in Europe that started around 900 years ago and lasted for 400 years. During the Middle Ages, trading and cities grew quickly.

Index

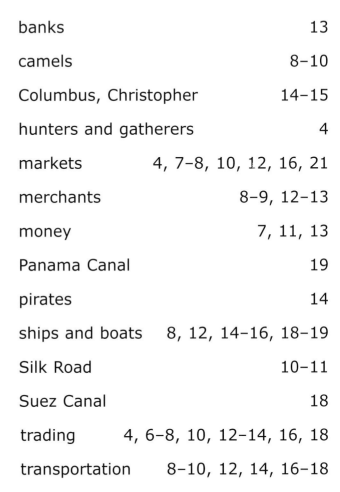

Discussion Starters

1 In the past, hunters and gatherers often had to travel long distances in search of food. Today, we can use a computer to order food. What are some good points about modern shopping? What are some bad points?

2 Today, we can buy food, clothes, and manufactured goods from around the world. Check the labels on your clothes. Where were they made? Why do you think we sometimes buy goods made in other countries?

3 Thanks to refrigeration, we can now buy strawberries at any time of the year. What other refrigerated goods can come from other countries?